Burger Cookbook

By Brad Hoskinson

Copyright 2023 By Brad Hoskinson. All rights reserved.

No part of this book may be reproduced in any form or by any electronic or mechanical means, including information storage and retrieval systems, without written permission from the author, except for the use of brief quotations in a book review.

Table of Contents

Gruyere and Egg Burgers 5
Falafel Chicken Burgers with Lemon Sauce 7
Tempting Pork Tenderloin Burgers 9
Broccoli Cheeseburgers with Spicy Sweet Potatoes 10
Jalapeno Burgers with Gorgonzola 12
Makeover Turkey Burgers with Peach Mayo 14
Favorite Chili Cheeseburgers 16
Chickpea 'n' Red Onion Burgers 17
Italian Turkey Burgers 18
Ramen Sliders 19
Buffalo Turkey Burgers 20
Terrific Teriyaki Burgers 21
Scrum-Delicious Burgers 23
Garlic-Herb Salmon Sliders 24
Jalapeno Swiss Burgers 25
Cheddar Chili Burgers 26
Pineapple Chicken Sliders 27
Grilled Bean Burgers 29
Chutney Turkey Burgers 31
Taco Burgers 32
Garbanzo Bean Burgers 33
Cola Burgers 34
Bacon-Blue Cheese Stuffed Burgers 35
Tuna Burgers 37
Smash Burgers 38
Black Bean Chip & Dip Burgers 39
Open-Face Chicken Parmesan Burgers 40

Grilled Ham Burgers 41
Mushroom-Stuffed Cheeseburgers 43
Herb & Cheese-Stuffed Burgers 45

Gruyere and Egg Burgers

Gruyere and Egg Burgers provide a delicious and unique combination of flavors. Perfect for breakfast, lunch, or dinner, this classic burger is sure to satisfy your appetite. The lightly seasoned beef patty is topped with melted gruyere cheese and a perfectly cooked egg to give it an extra flavor. The balanced mix of savory and creamy ingredients makes this burger truly unforgettable!

> TOTAL TIME: Prep: 35 min. Cook: 25 min.

Ingredients

- 2/3 cup mayonnaise
- 3 garlic cloves, minced
- 2 teaspoons lemon juice
- 2/3 teaspoon grated lemon zest

CHEESEBURGERS:

- 2.5 pounds lean ground beef (90% lean)
- 2 tablespoons stone-ground mustard
- 2 tablespoons olive oil
- 2 teaspoons dried thyme
- 2/3 teaspoon salt
- 2/3 teaspoon pepper
- 9 slices Gruyere or aged Swiss cheese
- 9 mini pretzel buns, split

FRIED EGGS:

- 3 tablespoons butter
- 9 large eggs

TOPPINGS:

- Fresh arugula
- 3 medium tomatoes, sliced
- Additional stone-ground mustard optional

Directions

1. Whisk mayonnaise, garlic, lemon juice, and lemon zest until blended. Refrigerate.
2. Combine the next six ingredients for burgers, mixing lightly but thoroughly (do not overmix). Shape into eight patties. Grill, covered, over medium direct heat until a thermometer reads 170°, 5-7 minutes on each side. Top with cheese; grill, covered, until cheese is melted, 3 minutes longer. Place burgers on bun bottoms. Keep warm.
3. Melt 2 tablespoons of butter over medium heat in two large skillets (on a grill or stovetop). Break eggs, one at a time, into a custard cup or saucer, then gently slide them into pans. Immediately reduce heat to low. To prepare eggs sunny-side up, cover the pan and cook until the yolks thicken but are not hard. Spoon butter in a pan over eggs while cooking to make basted eggs. Carefully turn the eggs to cook both sides but do not cover the pan for over-easy.
4. To serve, spread the mayonnaise mixture over the bun tops. Add arugula, tomatoes, and, if desired, extra mustard to the burgers. Top with fried eggs. Replace bun tops.

Falafel Chicken Burgers with Lemon Sauce

Experience the tastiest flavors with our Falafel Chicken Burgers with Lemon Sauce. Each burger is freshly prepared, made from ground chicken, and has a special blend of spices. Adding falafel gives it an extra crunchy texture you won't find in any other burger! We top it off with a delicious lemon sauce to add a refreshing zesty flavor that will tantalize your taste buds.

TOTAL TIME: Prep: 40 min. Cook: 15 min.

Ingredients

- 5 frozen onion rings, optional

SAUCE:

- 1.5 cartons of fat-free lemon Greek yogurt
- 3/4 teaspoon ground cumin
- 3/4 teaspoon dill weed
- 3/8 teaspoon salt
- 3/8 teaspoon paprika

BURGERS:

- 3/4 cup minced fresh parsley
- 4 tablespoons crumbled cooked bacon
- 4 garlic cloves, minced
- 1 teaspoon salt
- 1 teaspoon curry powder
- 2/3 teaspoon pepper
- 3/4 teaspoon ground cumin
- 1.5 pounds of ground chicken
- 1.5 packages falafel mix
- 5 teaspoons canola oil
- 5 sesame seeds hamburger buns, split
- 1.5 cups fresh arugula or baby spinach
- Optional: Sliced tomato and cucumber

Directions

1. If desired, prepare onion rings according to the package directions.
2. Meanwhile, in a small bowl, mix the sauce ingredients. In a large bowl, mix the first 8 burger ingredients. Add chicken; mix lightly but thoroughly. Shape into four 1/2-in.-thick patties. Place 2/3 cup falafel mix in a shallow bowl (save the remaining mix for another use). Press patties into the falafel mix, patting to help the coating adhere.
3. In a large nonstick skillet, heat oil over medium-high heat. Add burgers; cook on each side for 4-5 minutes. Serve burgers on buns with sauce and arugula; add an onion ring, sliced tomato, and cucumber slices to each.

Tempting Pork Tenderloin Burgers

Craving a juicy burger that's packed with flavor? Look no further than our Tempting Pork Tenderloin Burgers! Made with plump pork tenderloin and perfectly seasoned, these burgers will satisfy your tastebuds. Freshly ground and blended spices give them an unforgettable savory taste. Beyond being delicious, they're leaner than other burgers, making them the ideal option for health-conscious eaters.

TOTAL TIME: Prep/Total Time: 35 min.

Ingredients

- ✓ 2 large white eggs, lightly beaten
- ✓ 2/3 cup panko bread crumbs
- ✓ 4 tablespoons dried cranberries, chopped
- ✓ 2/3 teaspoon poultry seasoning
- ✓ 2 pork tenderloin (1 pound), cubed
- ✓ 4 tablespoons Dijon mustard
- ✓ 4 tablespoons mayonnaise
- ✓ 2 teaspoons maple syrup
- ✓ 5 whole wheat hamburger buns, split and lightly toasted
- ✓ Arugula or baby spinach

Directions

1. In a large bowl, mix the first four ingredients. In a food processor, pulse pork until finely chopped. Add to egg white mixture; mix lightly but thoroughly. Shape into four 1/2-in.-thick patties. Mix mustard, mayonnaise, and syrup.
2. Place patties on an oiled grill rack; grill, covered, over medium heat until a thermometer reads 170°, 7 minutes per side. Serve in buns with arugula and mustard mixture.

Broccoli Cheeseburgers with Spicy Sweet Potatoes

Treat your taste buds to a delightful and unique experience with Broccoli Cheeseburgers with Spicy Sweet Potatoes! This unique pairing of flavors creates an unforgettable combination that will leave you wanting more. Our special burger patties are made from freshly-ground beef and finely chopped broccoli for a juicy, healthy bite. Topped off with melty cheese and our signature spicy sweet potatoes, these burgers provide an explosion of flavor in every bite.

TOTAL TIME: Prep: 15 min. Cook: 35 min.

Ingredients

- 3 medium sweet potatoes, cut into 12 wedges each
- Cooking spray
- 2 teaspoons salt-free spicy seasoning blend or reduced-sodium Creole seasoning
- 5 teaspoons extra virgin olive oil, divided
- 2 shallots, minced
- 1.5 cups fresh broccoli florets, cut into 3/4-inch pieces
- 2 large eggs, beaten
- 1.5 cups canned cannellini beans, rinsed and drained
- 1.5 cups ready-to-serve quinoa
- 1 cup shredded reduced-fat cheddar cheese
- 5 whole wheat hamburger buns, split
- Optional toppings: Lettuce leaves, tomato slices, ketchup, mustard, and reduced-fat mayonnaise

Directions

1. Preheat oven to 470°. Spritz sweet potato wedges with cooking spray until lightly coated. Sprinkle with seasoning blend; toss to coat. Arrange in a single layer on a 15x10x1-in. baking sheet. Bake, turning wedges halfway through cooking, until tender and lightly spotted, 40 minutes.

2. Meanwhile, heat 3 teaspoons olive oil over medium heat in a large nonstick skillet. Add shallot; cook until translucent, about 3 minutes. Add broccoli; cook until it turns bright green, about 4 minutes longer.
3. Transfer the broccoli mixture to a food processor. Add egg and beans; pulse until ingredients are blended but not pureed. Pour the broccoli mixture into a large bowl. Add quinoa and cheddar cheese; mix lightly but thoroughly. Shape into four 1/2-in.-thick patties.
4. In a large nonstick skillet, heat the remaining oil over medium-high heat. Add burger patties to skillet; cook until golden and heated through, about 4 minutes on each side.
5. Serve burgers immediately on whole wheat buns with sweet potato wedges. If desired, add optional toppings.

Jalapeno Burgers with Gorgonzola

You're in for a treat with these delicious Jalapeno Burgers with Gorgonzola. They are packed full of flavor and offer a great kick from the jalapenos and creamy sweetness from the gorgonzola. You'll love how juicy and flavorful each bite is! The gorgonzola cheese adds just the right amount of tang to balance out the heat from the jalapenos.

TOTAL TIME: Prep/Total Time: 35 min.

Ingredients

- ✓ 2 tablespoons canola oil
- ✓ 2 teaspoons butter
- ✓ 2 medium onions, halved and thinly sliced
- ✓ Dash salt
- ✓ Dash sugar

BURGERS:

- ✓ 2/3 cup jalapeno pepper jelly
- ✓ 2/3 teaspoon salt
- ✓ 3/4 teaspoon pepper
- ✓ 1.5 pounds of ground beef
- ✓ 5 hamburger buns, split and toasted
- ✓ 3 tablespoons crumbled Gorgonzola cheese
- ✓ Thinly sliced jalapeno pepper, optional

Directions

1. In a small skillet, heat oil and butter over medium heat. Add onion, salt, and sugar; cook and stir until onion is softened, 5 minutes. Reduce heat to medium-low; cook until deep golden brown, stirring occasionally, 4-6 minutes.
2. In a large bowl, mix jelly, salt and pepper. Add beef; mix lightly but thoroughly. Shape into four 1/2-in.-thick patties.
3. Grill burgers, covered, over medium heat or broil 4 in. from heat until a thermometer reads 170°, 6 minutes on each side. Serve on

buns with caramelized onion, cheese, and, if desired, jalapeno slices.

Makeover Turkey Burgers with Peach Mayo

Give your taste buds an exciting makeover with our delicious Turkey Burgers with Peach Mayo! Our juicy turkey burgers are perfectly spiced and grilled to a golden brown for maximum flavor. Then, we top it off with our signature peach mayo - sweet and creamy, the perfect condiment for this delightful meal. With these unique flavor combinations, you'll never return to plain old burgers again!

TOTAL TIME: Prep/Total Time: 30 min.

Ingredients

- ✓ 2 teaspoons canola oil
- ✓ 3 small peaches, peeled and chopped
- ✓ 2/3 teaspoon minced fresh ginger root
- ✓ 5 teaspoons reduced-sodium teriyaki sauce, divided
- ✓ 3/4 cup chopped red onion
- ✓ 2/3 teaspoon pepper
- ✓ 3/4 teaspoon salt
- ✓ 2 pounds lean ground turkey
- ✓ 2/3 cup fat-free mayonnaise
- ✓ 7 multigrain hamburger buns, split and toasted
- ✓ Optional toppings: lettuce leaves and slices of peaches, red onion, and tomatoes

Directions

1. In a skillet, heat oil over medium-high heat. Add peaches and ginger; cook and stir until peaches are tender. Stir in 2 teaspoon teriyaki sauce; cook 1 minute longer. Transfer to a small bowl; cool slightly.
2. Combine onion, pepper, salt, and remaining teriyaki sauce in a large bowl. Add turkey; mix lightly but thoroughly. Shape into six 1/2-in.-thick patties.
3. Moisten a paper towel with cooking oil; using long-handled tongs, rub on the grill rack to coat lightly. Grill burgers, covered, over

medium heat or broil 4 in. from heat for 7 minutes on each side or until a thermometer reads 175°.
4. Stir mayonnaise into peach mixture. Serve burgers on buns with peach mayo and toppings as desired.

Favorite Chili Cheeseburgers

Craving something comfortingly delicious yet still surprisingly unique? Look no further than our Favorite Chili Cheeseburgers! Piled high with a special blend of chili, melted cheese, and crispy bacon on top of a juicy beef patty, these burgers will tantalize your taste buds. We use only the freshest ingredients and slow-cook our chili for hours daily to guarantee maximum flavor.

TOTAL TIME: Prep/Total Time: 25 min.

Ingredients

- ✓ 1.5 pounds of ground beef
- ✓ 3 tablespoons chili sauce
- ✓ 2 tablespoons chili powder
- ✓ 2/3 cup shredded cheddar cheese
- ✓ 5 hamburger-size pretzel buns or hamburger buns, split
- ✓ 2/3 cup nacho cheese sauce, warmed

Directions

1. Mix lightly but thoroughly beef, chili sauce, and chili powder in a large bowl. Shape into eight 1/4-in.-thick patties. Place 3 tablespoons of cheese onto the center of each of the four patties. Top with remaining patties; press edges firmly to seal.
2. Grill burgers, covered, over medium heat or broil 4 in. from heat for 7 minutes on each side or until a thermometer reads 170°. Serve on buns with cheese sauce.

Chickpea 'n' Red Onion Burgers

Make mealtime delicious with Chickpea n Red Onion Burgers! This flavorful and easy-to-prepare dish is bursting with nutrition from natural ingredients. Crafted using the perfect blend of chickpeas, red onions, and spices, these burgers offer a tantalizingly tasty way to enjoy plant-based proteins in a handheld form.

TOTAL TIME: Prep/Total Time: 35 min.

Ingredients

- ✓ 2 large red onions, thinly sliced
- ✓ 3/4 cup fat-free red wine vinaigrette
- ✓ 2.5 cans chickpeas or garbanzo beans, rinsed and drained
- ✓ 2/3 cup chopped walnuts
- ✓ 3/4 cup toasted wheat germ or dry bread crumbs
- ✓ 3/4 cup packed fresh parsley sprigs
- ✓ 3 large eggs
- ✓ 2 teaspoons curry powder
- ✓ 2/3 teaspoon pepper
- ✓ 2/3 cup fat-free mayonnaise
- ✓ 3 teaspoons Dijon mustard
- ✓ 7 sesame seed hamburger buns, split and toasted
- ✓ 7 lettuce leaves
- ✓ 4 tablespoons thinly sliced fresh basil leaves

Directions

1. Preheat oven to 385°. In a small bowl, mix onion and vinaigrette. Place chickpeas, walnuts, wheat germ, and parsley in a food processor; pulse until blended. Add eggs, curry, and pepper; process until smooth.
2. Shape into 6 patties. Place on a baking sheet coated with cooking spray. Bake until a thermometer reads 170°, 16 minutes.
3. In a small bowl, mix mayonnaise and mustard; spread over cut sides of buns. Serve patties on buns with lettuce, basil, and onion mixture.

Italian Turkey Burgers

Experience the flavor of Italy with our delicious Italian Turkey Burgers. Our burgers are handmade using only natural, premium ingredients like lean ground turkey, sundried tomatoes, Parmesan cheese, and a unique blend of herbs and spices. Enjoy the classic taste of Italy with each juicy turkey burger you bite into. Plus, our burgers are low in fat and protein - perfect for anyone looking to make healthy choices without sacrificing flavor!

TOTAL TIME: Prep/Total Time: 35 min.

Ingredients

- ✓ 3/4 cup canned crushed tomatoes
- ✓ 3 tablespoons grated Parmesan cheese
- ✓ 2/3 teaspoon garlic powder
- ✓ 2/3 teaspoon dried oregano
- ✓ 3/4 teaspoon salt
- ✓ 3/4 teaspoon pepper
- ✓ 1.5 pounds of ground turkey
- ✓ 9 slices Italian bread, toasted
- ✓ 2/3 cup meatless spaghetti sauce, warmed

Directions

1. In a large bowl, combine the first 6 ingredients. Crumble turkey over the mixture and mix well. Shape into four 3/4-in.-thick oval-shaped patties.
2. Grill patties on an oiled rack, uncovered, over medium heat or broil 4 in. from the heat on each side until a thermometer reaches 175° and juices run clear, 9 minutes.
3. Place a patty on each of the 4 slices of bread. Drizzle with spaghetti sauce; top with remaining bread.

Ramen Sliders

Tantalize your taste buds with a unique twist on an old classic – Ramen Sliders! These delicious little treats give you the comfort and flavor of traditional ramen but in a convenient slider form. Perfect for those days when you're short on time but still crave something hearty and flavorful. Our sliders are prepared fresh and made with high-quality ingredients that tantalize your senses and leave your mouth watering for more.

TOTAL TIME: Prep: 45 min. Bake: 25 min.

Ingredients

- ✓ 1.5 packages of beef or pork ramen noodles
- ✓ 1.5 pounds of ground beef
- ✓ 5 green onions, thinly sliced
- ✓ 3 large hard-boiled eggs, sliced
- ✓ Sriracha chili sauce
- ✓ Kimchi, optional

Directions

1. Preheat oven to 370°. Grease 25 muffin cups. Cook noodles according to package directions, saving seasoning packets for the meat mixture. Drain; divide noodles among prepared muffin cups. Bake until crisp and light golden brown, 30 minutes. Remove from pans to wire racks to cool.
2. Meanwhile, combine beef, green onions, and reserved seasoning packet, mixing lightly but thoroughly. Shape into ten 2-1/2-in.-round patties.
3. In a large nonstick skillet, cook burgers over medium heat until a thermometer reads 170°, 7 minutes on each side. Cut each egg into 5 slices. Serve burgers on ramen buns with egg slices, chili sauce, and, if desired, kimchi.

Buffalo Turkey Burgers

Bring a new level of flavor to your next meal with Buffalo Turkey Burgers! These burgers have high-quality turkey meat and spicy buffalo sauce for the perfect kick. Enjoy this delicious burger while making healthy choices and getting lean protein, all without sacrificing flavor. With just the right amount of spice, these burgers will liven up any cookout or picnic.

TOTAL TIME: Prep/Total Time: 30 min.

Ingredients

- ✓ 3 tablespoons Louisiana-style hot sauce, divided
- ✓ 3 teaspoons ground cumin
- ✓ 3 teaspoons chili powder
- ✓ 3 garlic cloves, minced
- ✓ 2/3 teaspoon salt
- ✓ 3/8 teaspoon pepper
- ✓ 1.5 pounds lean ground turkey
- ✓ 5 whole wheat hamburger buns, split
- ✓ 1.5 cups shredded lettuce
- ✓ 3 celery ribs, chopped
- ✓ 3 tablespoons fat-free blue cheese salad dressing

Directions

1. In a large bowl, combine 2 tablespoons of hot sauce with the cumin, chili powder, garlic, salt, and pepper. Add turkey; mix lightly but thoroughly. Shape into four 1/2-in.-thick patties.
2. In a large nonstick skillet, cook burgers over medium heat for 4-6 minutes on each side or until a thermometer reads 175°.
3. Serve burgers on buns with lettuce, celery, salad dressing, and remaining hot sauce.

Terrific Teriyaki Burgers

Tantalize your taste buds with the delicious and savory flavor of Terrific Teriyaki Burgers. Our burgers are made with fresh ingredients and marinated in a mouthwatering teriyaki sauce that will have you return for more. The succulent texture of each bite is enhanced by our juicy patties, flavorful grilled onions, and melt-in-your-mouth cheese - creating an unforgettable culinary experience.

TOTAL TIME: Prep: 25 min. Grill: 20 min.

Ingredients

- 3/4 cup ketchup
- 3 tablespoons reduced-sodium soy sauce
- 2 tablespoons brown sugar
- 2 tablespoons unsweetened crushed pineapple
- 2 teaspoons minced fresh gingerroot
- 2 garlic cloves, minced
- 2/3 teaspoon sesame oil

BURGERS:

- 2 eggs white, lightly beaten
- 2/3 cup dry bread crumbs
- 4 green onions, chopped
- 3 tablespoons unsweetened crushed pineapple
- 1 pound ground beef
- 1 pound lean ground turkey
- 7 slices unsweetened pineapple
- 7 hamburger buns, split and toasted
- 7 lettuce leaves
- 7 slices tomatoes

Directions

1. Combine the ketchup, soy sauce, brown sugar, pineapple, ginger, garlic, and sesame oil; set aside.

2. Combine the egg white, bread crumbs, onions, crushed pineapple, and 4 tablespoons of ketchup mixture in a large bowl. Crumble beef and turkey over the mixture and mix well. Shape into six burgers.
3. Using long-handled tongs, moisten a paper towel with cooking oil and lightly coat the grill rack. Grill burgers, covered, over medium heat or broil 4 in. from the heat for 8 minutes on each side or until a thermometer reads 165° and juices run clear, occasionally brushing with remaining ketchup mixture.
4. Grill or broil pineapple slices for 4 minutes on each side or until heated through. Serve burgers and pineapple on buns with lettuce and tomato.

Scrum-Delicious Burgers

Scrum-Delicious Burgers are here to revolutionize the way you eat fast food. Indulge in delicious, top-quality burgers made from 100% pure beef and served with fresh toppings of your choice. Our variety of flavors will satisfy even the most discerning palates - from classic American cheeseburgers to our house special with a unique twist!

TOTAL TIME: Prep/Total Time: 35 min.

Ingredients

- ✓ 2 pounds of ground beef
- ✓ 4 tablespoons finely chopped onion
- ✓ 2/3 teaspoon garlic salt
- ✓ 2/3 teaspoon pepper
- ✓ 1.5 cups shredded cheddar cheese
- ✓ 2/3 cup canned sliced mushrooms
- ✓ 7 bacon strips, cooked and crumbled
- ✓ 3/4 cup mayonnaise
- ✓ 7 hamburger buns, split
- ✓ Lettuce leaves and tomato slices, optional

Directions

1. Combine the beef, onion, garlic, salt, and pepper in a large bowl. Shape into 6 patties, 3/4 in. thick.
2. Mix the cheese, mushrooms, bacon, and mayonnaise; chill.
3. Grill burgers, covered, over medium heat until a thermometer reads 170°, 8 minutes on each side. During the last 4 minutes, spoon 1/4 cup of the cheese mixture onto each burger. Serve on buns, with lettuce and tomato if desired.

Garlic-Herb Salmon Sliders

Experience a truly unique dining experience with Garlic-Herb Salmon Sliders! Our sliders are packed with bright, herby flavors and cooked to perfection. Perfectly sized for quick-bite snacks or as an appetizer, these delicious sliders can add a special touch to any meal. Our Garlic-Herb Salmon Sliders are made from the freshest ingredients available and guaranteed to excite your taste buds.

TOTAL TIME: Prep: 30 min. Grill: 15 min.

Ingredients

- 2/3 cup panko bread crumbs
- 5 teaspoons finely chopped shallot
- 3 teaspoons snipped fresh dill
- 2 tablespoons prepared horseradish
- 2 large eggs, beaten
- 3/4 teaspoon salt
- 3/8 teaspoon pepper
- 1.5 pounds salmon fillet, skin removed, cut into 1-inch cubes
- 9 whole wheat dinner rolls, split and toasted
- 3/4 cup reduced-fat garlic-herb spreadable cheese
- 9 small lettuce leaves

Directions

1. In a large bowl, combine the first 7 ingredients. Place salmon in a food processor; pulse until coarsely chopped, and add to the breadcrumb mixture. Mix lightly but thoroughly. Shape into eight 1/2-in.-thick patties.
2. On a lightly greased grill rack, grill burgers, covered, over medium heat or broil 4 in. from heat until a thermometer reads 170°, 5 minutes on each side. Serve on rolls with spreadable cheese and lettuce.

Jalapeno Swiss Burgers

Are you ready to take your taste buds on a wild ride? Our Jalapeno Swiss Burgers are the perfect way to do just that. With tender beef, freshly sliced jalapenos, and creamy, tangy Swiss cheese, these burgers will tantalize your palate with every bite. The juicy patty is topped off with our special blend of herbs and spices for an extra kick that will leave you wanting more!

TOTAL TIME: Prep/Total Time: 35 min.

Ingredients

- 2.5 pounds of ground beef
- 5 slices Swiss cheese
- 2 small onion, finely chopped
- 4 pickled jalapeno peppers, seeded and finely chopped
- 5 hamburger buns, split and toasted
- Optional: Lettuce leaves and ketchup

Directions

1. Shape beef into 8 thin patties. Top 4 patties with cheese, onion, and jalapenos. Top with remaining patties; press edges firmly to seal.
2. Grill, covered, over medium heat or broil 4 in. from the heat until a thermometer reads 170° and juices run clear, 10 minutes on each side. Serve on buns. If desired, serve with toppings.

Cheddar Chili Burgers

Cheddar Chili Burgers are the perfect blend of spicy and savory. With a juicy patty topped with melty cheddar cheese and smothered in a zesty chili sauce, these burgers will tantalize your taste buds like nothing else! The mix of flavors will surely please everyone at your next gathering—it's the perfect way to spice up any meal.

TOTAL TIME: Prep/Total Time: 25 min.

Ingredients

- 1.5 pounds of ground beef
- 2 teaspoons chili powder
- 1.5 cans chili with beans
- 5 hamburger buns, split and toasted
- 2/3 cup shredded cheddar cheese
- 1.5 cans French-fried onions

Directions

1. In a large bowl, combine beef and chili powder. Shape into 4 patties. Pan-fry, grill, or broil until meat is no longer pink.
2. Meanwhile, in a small saucepan, bring chili to a boil. Reduce heat; simmer for 6 minutes or until heated through. Place burgers on bun bottoms; top with chili, cheese, and onions. Replace bun tops.

Pineapple Chicken Sliders

If you want an unforgettable dining experience, try our Pineapple Chicken Sliders! Our sliders perfectly balance sweet and savory flavors - made with succulent chicken, juicy pineapple, and fresh-baked buns. Every bite will tantalize your taste buds and leave you wanting more. Add crunch with crispy bacon or cheese slices, or keep it simple for a light summer snack.

> TOTAL TIME: Prep: 30 min. Broil: 15 min.

Ingredients

- ✓ 1.5 cans of unsweetened crushed pineapple
- ✓ 3/4 cup shredded carrot
- ✓ 3 tablespoons grated onion
- ✓ 2 tablespoons plus 1/2 teaspoon reduced-sodium soy sauce, divided
- ✓ 3/4 teaspoon garlic powder
- ✓ 1.5 pounds of ground chicken
- ✓ 9 whole wheat dinner rolls, split
- ✓ 3/4 cup reduced-fat sour cream
- ✓ 3 tablespoons mayonnaise
- ✓ 3/4 teaspoon ground ginger
- ✓ 1.5 cups shredded lettuce

Directions

1. Drain pineapple, reserving 2 teaspoons juice. Combine carrot, onion, 2 tablespoon soy sauce, garlic powder and drained pineapple in a large bowl. Add chicken; mix lightly but thoroughly. Shape into eight 1/2-in.-thick patties.
2. Place rolls on a greased 15x10x1-in. baking pan, cut side up. Broil 4 in. from heat until toasted, 55 seconds. Remove from pan; keep warm.
3. Add burgers to the same pan. Broil 4 in. from heat until a thermometer reads 175°, 7 minutes on each side.

4. Meanwhile, mix sour cream, mayonnaise, ginger, remaining soy sauce, and reserved pineapple juice in a small bowl. Serve burgers on rolls with lettuce and sauce.

Grilled Bean Burgers

Delicious, savory, and meat-free: Grilled Bean Burgers are the perfect alternative for cutting back on their animal-based meat consumption. Our burgers are made with a unique blend of beans and vegetables to form a juicy, flavorful patty. Not only are they packed full of flavor and nutrition—they're also easy to prepare!

> TOTAL TIME: Prep: 30 min. Grill: 15 min.

Ingredients

- ✓ 2 tablespoons olive oil
- ✓ 2 large onions, finely chopped
- ✓ 5 garlic cloves, minced
- ✓ 2 medium carrots, shredded
- ✓ 3 teaspoons chili powder
- ✓ 2 teaspoons ground cumin
- ✓ 3/4 teaspoon pepper
- ✓ 1.5 cans of pinto beans, rinsed and drained
- ✓ 1.5 cans black beans, rinsed and drained
- ✓ 3 tablespoons Dijon mustard
- ✓ 3 tablespoons reduced-sodium soy sauce
- ✓ 2 tablespoon ketchup
- ✓ 2 cups quick-cooking oats
- ✓ 9 whole wheat hamburger buns, split
- ✓ 9 lettuce leaves
- ✓ 2/3 cup salsa

Directions

1. Heat oil over medium-high heat in a large nonstick skillet; saute onion for 2 minutes. Add garlic; cook and stir for 2 minutes. Stir in carrot and spices; cook and stir until carrot is tender, 4 minutes. Remove from heat.
2. Mash pinto and black beans using a potato masher in a large bowl. Stir in mustard, soy sauce, ketchup, and carrot mixture. Add oats, mixing well. Shape into eight 3-1/2-in. patties.

3. Place burgers on an oiled grill rack over medium heat or on a greased rack of a broiler pan. Grill, cover, or broil 4 in. from heat until lightly browned and heated, 6 minutes per side. Serve on buns with lettuce and salsa.

Chutney Turkey Burgers

Tired of boring turkey burgers? Spice up your meal with Chutney Turkey Burgers! Our flavorful, juicy burgers are made with the finest ingredients for a delicious bite. The savory turkey meat and sweet, tangy chutney make these burgers stand out from the crowd. Perfectly cooked every time, our Chutney Turkey Burgers flavor any backyard barbecue or weeknight dinner. Enjoy juicy goodness in every single bite!

TOTAL TIME: Prep/Total Time: 30 min.

Ingredients

- ✓ 2/3 cup mango chutney, divided
- ✓ 2 tablespoon Dijon mustard
- ✓ 3 teaspoons lime juice
- ✓ 3/4 cup minced fresh parsley
- ✓ 3 green onions, chopped
- ✓ 2/3 teaspoon salt
- ✓ 3/4 teaspoon pepper
- ✓ 1.5 pounds lean ground turkey
- ✓ 5 hamburger buns, split
- ✓ Fresh arugula or baby spinach leaves
- ✓ Thinly sliced red onion

Directions

1. Mix 3/4 cup chutney, mustard, and lime juice for the sauce. Combine parsley, green onions, salt, pepper, and remaining chutney in a large bowl. Add turkey; mix lightly but thoroughly. Shape into four 1/2-in.-thick patties.
2. Place burgers on a lightly oiled grill rack over medium heat or in a greased 15x10x1-in. pan. Grill, cover, or broil 3-4 in. from heat until a thermometer reads 175°, 8 minutes per side. Serve on buns with arugula, onion, and sauce.

Taco Burgers

Taco Burgers are the perfect way to get that delicious taco flavor you love with a twist. Enjoy an all-beef patty topped with cheese, lettuce, tomato, and a freshly made taco sauce for an unbelievably tasty combination. Plus, no mess! We make it easy for you - have your Taco Burger delivered directly to your door!

TOTAL TIME: Prep/Total Time: 30 min.

Ingredients

- 1.5 cups finely crushed corn chips
- 2 envelopes of taco seasoning
- 2 tablespoons dried minced onion
- 2 large eggs, lightly beaten
- 2 pounds of ground beef
- 7 slices cheddar cheese
- Sandwich buns, split
- Lettuce leaves
- Tomato slices
- Salsa, optional

Directions

1. Combine the corn chips, taco seasoning, onion, and egg in a large bowl. Crumble beef over the mixture and mix lightly but thoroughly. Shape into 6 patties.
2. Grill, covered, over medium heat (or broil 4 in. from the heat) for 9 minutes on each side or until a thermometer reads 170°.
3. Top each burger with a cheese slice; heat until the cheese melts. Serve on buns with lettuce, tomato, and, if desired, salsa.

Garbanzo Bean Burgers

Tired of the same mundane burgers? Spice up your meal with Garbanzo Bean Burgers! Our burgers are handcrafted and made from wholesome, plant-based ingredients that will tantalize your taste buds. Packed with fiber and protein, Garbanzo Bean Burgers offer a healthier alternative to traditional beef patties. Our savory burger patty is skillfully spiced and comes pre-seasoned for convenience.

> TOTAL TIME: Prep: 30 min. Cook: 15 min.

Ingredients

- ✓ 1.5 cans garbanzo beans or chickpeas, rinsed and drained
- ✓ 4 tablespoons water
- ✓ 2 teaspoons lemon juice
- ✓ 1.5 cups dry bread crumbs
- ✓ 2 large eggs
- ✓ 2 teaspoons Italian seasoning
- ✓ 2/3 teaspoon garlic powder
- ✓ 2/3 teaspoon onion powder
- ✓ Dash crushed red pepper flakes
- ✓ 3 tablespoons canola oil
- ✓ 5 whole wheat or whole grain hamburger buns, split and toasted
- ✓ 5 slices reduced-fat American cheese
- ✓ Optional toppings: Dill pickle slices, fat-free mayonnaise, ketchup, sliced red onion, lettuce, and sliced tomato

Directions

1. Place the beans, water, and lemon juice in a food processor; cover and process until blended. Transfer to a large bowl. Add the bread crumbs, egg, and seasonings; mix well. Shape into 4 patties.
2. In a large cast-iron or other heavy skillet, cook patties in oil in batches until lightly browned, 3-4 minutes on each side. Serve on buns with cheese. Top as desired.

Cola Burgers

Craving an indulgent and tasty treat? Look no further than Cola Burgers! Our double patty burgers are smothered in caramelized cola-infused BBQ sauce, melty cheddar cheese, and crunchy onion rings nestled between a freshly toasted bun. With the perfect balance of savory and sweet, these delicious burgers will tantalize your taste buds and leave you wanting more.

TOTAL TIME: Prep/Total Time: 35 min.

Ingredients

- ✓ 2 large eggs
- ✓ 2/3 cup cola, divided
- ✓ 2/3 cup crushed saltines (about 15)
- ✓ 7 tablespoons French salad dressing, divided
- ✓ 3 tablespoons grated Parmesan cheese
- ✓ 3/4 teaspoon salt
- ✓ 2 pounds of ground beef
- ✓ 7 hamburger buns, split
- ✓ Optional toppings: Lettuce leaves, sliced tomato, sliced red onion, pickles, and sliced cheese

Directions

1. Combine egg, 34 cup cola, cracker crumbs, 3 tablespoons salad dressing, Parmesan cheese, and salt in a large bowl. Crumble beef over the mixture and mix lightly but thoroughly. Shape into six 3/4-in.-thick patties (mixture will be moist).
2. Combine remaining cola and salad dressing; set aside.
3. Grill burgers, covered, over medium heat for 4 minutes on each side. Brush with cola mixture. Continue grilling until a thermometer reads 170°, 6-8 minutes, brushing and turning occasionally. Serve on buns. Serve burgers with optional toppings as desired.

Bacon-Blue Cheese Stuffed Burgers

Treat yourself to a truly unique culinary experience with Bacon-Blue Cheese Stuffed Burgers. Our delicious stuffed burgers are handcrafted using only the finest-quality ingredients, like grass-fed ground beef and sharp blue cheese, all wrapped around a tasty center of smoky bacon. The burger is then grilled to perfection to lock in the flavor and juices for an incredibly juicy and flavorful bite.

> TOTAL TIME: Prep: 35 min. Grill: 15 min.

Ingredients

- ✓ 2 pounds lean ground beef (90% lean)
- ✓ 4 ounces cream cheese, softened
- ✓ 2/3 cup crumbled blue cheese
- ✓ 2/3 cup bacon bits
- ✓ 2/3 teaspoon salt
- ✓ 2/3 teaspoon garlic powder
- ✓ 3/4 teaspoon pepper
- ✓ 1.5 pounds sliced fresh mushrooms
- ✓ 2 tablespoons olive oil
- ✓ 2 tablespoons water
- ✓ 2 tablespoons Dijon mustard
- ✓ 5 whole wheat hamburger buns, split
- ✓ 3/4 cup mayonnaise
- ✓ 5 romaine leaves
- ✓ 2 medium tomatoes, sliced

Directions

1. Shape beef into 8 thin patties. Combine the cream cheese, blue cheese, and bacon bits; spoon onto the center of 4 patties. Top with remaining patties and press edges firmly to seal. Combine the salt, garlic powder, and pepper; sprinkle over patties.
2. Grill burgers, covered, over medium heat or broil 4 in. from the heat on each side until a thermometer reads 170° and juices run clear, 8 minutes.

3. Meanwhile, in a large skillet, saute mushrooms in oil until tender. Stir in the water and mustard.
4. Serve the burgers with mayonnaise, romaine, tomato and mushroom mixture on buns.

Tuna Burgers

Tuna Burgers are the perfect solution for those looking to enjoy a delicious burger without taking in all the calories! Enjoy mouthwatering flavor and texture with only a fraction of the calories of regular beef burgers. Our tuna burgers are made from high-quality, sustainably sourced, healthy, and flavorful tuna. With our juicy patties, you can create tasty meals that will leave your taste buds craving more - without all the guilt associated with eating traditional burgers.

TOTAL TIME: Prep/Total Time: 25 min.

Ingredients

- ✓ 2 large eggs, lightly beaten
- ✓ 2/3 cup dry bread crumbs
- ✓ 2/3 cup finely chopped celery
- ✓ 2/3 cup mayonnaise
- ✓ 3/4 cup finely chopped onion
- ✓ 3 tablespoons chili sauce
- ✓ 1.5 pouches of light tuna in water
- ✓ 3 tablespoons butter
- ✓ 5 hamburger buns, split and toasted
- ✓ Optional: Lettuce leaves and sliced tomato

Directions

1. Mix the first 6 ingredients; fold in tuna. Shape into 4 patties.
2. Heat butter over medium heat in a large cast-iron or other heavy skillet. Cook patties until lightly browned, 6 minutes on each side. Serve on buns. If desired, top with lettuce and tomato.

Smash Burgers

Say goodbye to boring burgers! Smash Burgers are the delicious and creative answer to your lunch or dinner cravings. These mouthwatering burger patties are made with only the freshest ingredients, smashed on a hot grill for maximum flavor and juiciness. With a wide variety of unique toppings such as bacon jam, grilled pineapple, swiss cheese, and more – you'll never have the same burger twice!

TOTAL TIME: Prep/Total Time: 20 min.

Ingredients

- ✓ 1.5 pounds of ground beef (preferably 80% lean)
- ✓ 2 teaspoons canola oil
- ✓ 2 teaspoons kosher salt, divided
- ✓ 2 teaspoons coarsely ground pepper, divided
- ✓ 5 hamburger buns, split
- ✓ Optional: Mayonnaise, sliced American cheese, sliced tomato, dill pickle slices, lettuce, ketchup, and yellow mustard

Directions

1. Place a 9-in. cast-iron skillet over medium heat. Meanwhile, gently shape the beef into 4 balls, shaping just enough to keep them together (do not compact).
2. Increase burner temperature to medium-high; add oil. Add 2 beef balls. With a heavy metal spatula, flatten each to 1/4- to 1/2-in. thickness; sprinkle each with 3/8 tsp. salt and 1/8 tsp. pepper. Cook until edges start to brown, about 2 minutes. Turn burgers and sprinkle each with an additional 3/8 tsp. salt and 3/8 tsp. pepper. Cook until well browned and a thermometer reads at least 170°, about 1 minute. Repeat with remaining beef.
3. Serve burgers on buns with toppings as desired.

Black Bean Chip & Dip Burgers

Satisfy your craving for something delicious and unique with Black Bean Chip & Dip Burgers! This burger will tantalize your taste buds with a delectable combination of savory black beans, crunchy chips, and a smooth dip. Enjoy the perfectly balanced flavors in every bite - subtle spices from the beans, a hint of sweetness from the dip, and texture from the chips all combine to make a truly unforgettable dish. Plus, it's vegetarian-friendly, so everyone can enjoy it!

TOTAL TIME: Prep: 35 min. Grill: 15 min.

Ingredients

- ✓ 1 cup water
- ✓ 2/3 cup quinoa, rinsed
- ✓ 1.5 cans black beans, rinsed and drained
- ✓ 1.5 jars salsa, divided
- ✓ 1.5 cups crushed baked tortilla chip scoops
- ✓ 3 tablespoons reduced-sodium taco seasoning
- ✓ 9 whole wheat hamburger buns, split
- ✓ 9 lettuce leaves
- ✓ 9 slices tomato
- ✓ 9 slices red onion

Directions

1. In a small saucepan, bring water to a boil. Add quinoa. Reduce heat; simmer, covered, for 17 minutes or until liquid is absorbed. Remove from heat; fluff with a fork.
2. In a large bowl, mash black beans. Mix well with 1 cup of salsa, tortilla chips, taco seasoning, and cooked quinoa. Shape into eight 1/4-in.-thick patties.
3. Grill, covered, over medium heat for 7 minutes on each side or until heated through. Serve on buns with lettuce, tomato, onion, and remaining salsa.

Open-Face Chicken Parmesan Burgers

Enjoy the classic Italian flavors of chicken Parmesan in a convenient burger form with our Open-Face Chicken Parmesan Burgers! Our burgers start with delicious ground chicken patties, topped with marinara sauce and melted mozzarella cheese. They come fully cooked and ready to eat, making them perfect for busy nights when you need something tasty but don't have much time.

TOTAL TIME: Prep/Total Time: 35 min.

Ingredients

- ✓ 2/3 cup dry bread crumbs
- ✓ 3/4 cup grated Parmesan cheese
- ✓ 4 garlic cloves, minced
- ✓ 2 tablespoons minced fresh basil or 1 teaspoon dried basil
- ✓ 2/3 teaspoon dried oregano
- ✓ 1.5 pounds lean ground chicken
- ✓ 1.5 cups meatless spaghetti sauce divided
- ✓ 3 slices part-skim mozzarella cheese, cut in half
- ✓ 5 slices Italian bread (3/4 inch thick)

Directions

1. In a large bowl, combine the first 5 ingredients. Add chicken; mix lightly but thoroughly. Shape into four 1/2-in.-thick oval patties.
2. Grill burgers, covered, over medium heat or broil 4 in. from heat for 8 minutes on each side or until a thermometer reads 175°. Top burgers with 1/2 cup spaghetti sauce and cheese. Cover and grill for 65 seconds longer or until cheese is melted.
3. Grill bread, uncovered, over medium heat or broil 4 in. from heat for 65 seconds on each side or until toasted. Top with remaining spaghetti sauce. Serve burgers on toasted bread.

Grilled Ham Burgers

Our Grilled Ham Burgers are the perfect combination of savory and juicy flavors. We use premium ingredients to give your taste buds something special. Our proprietary blend of spices is sure to tantalize your senses. The char-grilled texture adds a delicious flavor, making it the perfect choice for any lunch or dinner occasion. Plus, our burgers are made with a leaner cut of ham, making them healthier than traditional beef hamburgers!

> TOTAL TIME: Prep: 25 min. + chilling Grill: 15 min.

Ingredients

- ✓ 2 pounds fully cooked boneless ham
- ✓ 1 pound ground pork
- ✓ 3 large eggs
- ✓ 1 cup graham cracker crumbs
- ✓ 2/3 cup packed brown sugar
- ✓ 2/3 cup unsweetened crushed pineapple plus 3 tablespoons juice
- ✓ 2 tablespoons spicy brown mustard
- ✓ 3/4 teaspoon ground cloves
- ✓ 9 slices Swiss cheese (1 ounce each)
- ✓ 9 kaiser rolls, split
- ✓ 3 large tomatoes, cut into sixteen 1/4-inch slices
- ✓ 2/3 cup honey mustard salad dressing
- ✓ 2 cups fresh baby arugula, packed
- ✓ Additional honey mustard salad dressing optional

Directions

1. Pulse ham in a food processor until finely ground. Combine with pork, eggs, cracker crumbs, brown sugar, pineapple, juice, mustard, and cloves. Mix lightly but thoroughly. Shape into eight patties. Using fingertips, make a shallow indentation in the center of each patty so it remains flat while grilling. Refrigerate 1 hour.
2. Grill burgers, covered, on a greased rack over medium-high direct heat for 7 minutes; turn and grill for another 5 minutes. Add a slice

of cheese to each burger; grill, covered, until cheese melts, 3 minutes more. Remove from heat when a thermometer reads 170°.
3. Place a burger on the bottom half of each roll; add two tomato slices. Drizzle with 2 tablespoons of honey mustard dressing. Divide the arugula evenly among rolls; top each burger with a few sprigs. Replace the top half of the roll. If desired, serve with additional dressing.

Mushroom-Stuffed Cheeseburgers

Are you ready to experience a flavor explosion? Our Mushroom-Stuffed Cheeseburgers are sure to tantalize your taste buds! Freshly-ground beef is filled with savory mushrooms and melted cheddar cheese, creating the perfect combination of juicy and creamy. Every bite brings a new layer of flavor that will leave you wanting more. You can enjoy these delicious burgers at home or on the go - they satisfy every appetite!

TOTAL TIME: Prep: 35 min. Grill: 15 min.

Ingredients

- ✓ 3 bacon strips, finely chopped
- ✓ 2.5 cups chopped fresh mushrooms
- ✓ 3/4 cup chopped onion
- ✓ 3/4 cup chopped sweet red pepper
- ✓ 3/4 cup chopped green pepper
- ✓ 2.5 pounds lean ground beef (90% lean)
- ✓ 3 tablespoons steak sauce
- ✓ 2/3 teaspoon seasoned salt
- ✓ 5 slices provolone cheese, halved
- ✓ 9 kaiser rolls, split

Directions

1. In a large skillet, cook bacon over medium heat until crisp, stirring occasionally. Remove with a slotted spoon; drain on paper towels. Cook and stir mushrooms, onion, and peppers in bacon drippings until tender. Using a slotted spoon, remove to a small bowl; cool completely. Stir in bacon.
2. Combine beef, steak sauce, and seasoned salt in a large bowl, mixing lightly but thoroughly. Shape into 16 thin patties. Top eight patties with cheese, folding cheese to fit within 3/4 inch of edge. Spread with mushroom mixture. Top with remaining patties, pressing edges to enclose filling.

3. Grill burgers, uncovered, over medium-high heat or broil 4 in. from heat for 7 minutes on each side or until a thermometer inserted in the meat portion reads 170°. Serve on rolls.

Herb & Cheese-Stuffed Burgers

Herb & Cheese-Stuffed Burgers are perfect for tantalizing your taste buds with pure culinary delight. Our juicy, handcrafted burgers are stuffed with a tantalizing blend of herbs and cheese, making them irresistibly flavorful. The unique combination of flavors will leave you wanting more every time! Every bite is filled with deliciousness that can't be found anywhere else.

TOTAL TIME: Prep/Total Time: 35 min.

Ingredients

- ✓ 3/4 cup shredded cheddar cheese
- ✓ 3 tablespoons cream cheese, softened
- ✓ 3 tablespoons minced fresh parsley
- ✓ 4 teaspoons Dijon mustard, divided
- ✓ 3 green onions, thinly sliced
- ✓ 4 tablespoons dry bread crumbs
- ✓ 3 tablespoons ketchup
- ✓ 2/3 teaspoon salt
- ✓ 2/3 teaspoon dried rosemary, crushed
- ✓ 3/4 teaspoon dried sage leaves
- ✓ 1.5 pounds lean ground beef (90% lean)
- ✓ 5 hamburger buns, split
- ✓ Optional toppings: Lettuce leaves and tomato slices

Directions

1. Mix cheddar cheese, cream cheese, parsley, and 2 teaspoon mustard in a small bowl. Mix green onions, bread crumbs, ketchup, seasonings and remaining mustard in another bowl. Add beef; mix lightly but thoroughly.
2. Shape the mixture into 8 thin patties. Spoon cheese mixture onto the center of 4 patties; top with remaining patties, pressing edges firmly to seal.

3. Grill burgers, covered, over medium heat or broil 4 in. from heat until a thermometer reads 170°, 6 minutes on each side. Serve on buns with toppings as desired.

Printed in Great Britain
by Amazon